STRENGTHENING POPULAR PARTICIPATION IN THE AFRICAN UNION

A Guide to AU Structures and Processes

Oxfam

AfriMAP

An Open Society Institute Network Publication

In memory of
Tajudeen Abdul Raheem
Pan-Africanist
1961–2009

First published in 2009 by the Open Society Initiative for Southern Africa (OSISA) and Oxfam
2nd impression 2010, with minor corrections

ISBN (paperback): 978-1-920355-24-1
ISBN (Ebrary): 978-1-920489-75-5
ISBN (MyiLibrary): 978-1-920489-76-2
ISBN (Adobe PDF digital edition): 978-1-920489-77-9

Produced by COMPRESS.dsl www.compressdsl.com

Distributed by
African Minds
4 Eccleston Place, Somerset West, 7130, South Africa
info@africanminds.co.za
www.africanminds.co.za

ORDERS:
African Books Collective
PO Box 721, Oxford OX1 9EN, UK
orders@africanbookscollective.com
www.africanbookscollective.com

Contents

Acknowledgements

This guide was researched and written by Rudo Chitiga, a development policy consultant, and Bronwen Manby, of the Open Society Institute's Africa Governance Monitoring and Advocacy Project (AfriMAP), with important contributions from Irũngũ Houghton, Pan-Africa Director, Oxfam, as well as Ibrahima Kane, Nobuntu Mbelle, Achieng Akena, Desiré Assogbavi, Pascal Kambale, Dismas Nkunda, Ozias Tungwarara, Dolphine Ndeda and Mary Anne Fitzgerald.

Much of the information in this guide is drawn from the report *Towards a People-Driven African Union: Current Obstacles and New Opportunities* (AfriMAP, AFRODAD and Oxfam, January 2007, updated November 2007) available on the websites of the publishing organisations. Additional information is derived from the report of the *Audit of the African Union* presented to Heads of State and Government in January 2008. The drafting of the guide was also enriched by a workshop organised in April 2007 in Accra by the Institute for Democratic Governance (IDEG), Ghana, and Oxfam with the support of Oxfam Novib.

Thanks to all those who offered lessons and insights on how civil society organisations can work more effectively to engage and influence the African Union and its various organs.

All contributions in the form of case studies, comments and updates on the issues included in this guide are greatly appreciated: please send to info@afrimap.org.

Acronyms

AEC	African Economic Community
APRM	African Peer Review Mechanism
AU	African Union
CIDO	African Citizens' and Diaspora Directorate (of the AU Commission)
CSO	Civil society organisation
ECOSOCC	Economic, Social and Cultural Council
EU	European Union
G8	'Group of eight' industrialised countries
NEPAD	New Partnership for Africa's Development
NGO	Non-governmental organisation
OAU	Organisation of African Unity
PAP	Pan-African Parliament
PRC	Permanent Representatives Council
PSC	Peace and Security Council
REC	Regional Economic Community
UN	United Nations

Introduction
The purpose of this guide

The African Union (AU) has committed to a vision of Africa that is 'integrated, prosperous and peaceful ... driven by its own citizens, a dynamic force in the global arena' (*Vision and Mission of the African Union*, May 2004).

This guide is an effort to take up the challenge of achieving this vision. It is a tool to assist activists to engage with AU policies and programmes. It describes the AU decision-making process and outlines the roles and responsibilities of the AU institutions. It also contains a sampling of the experiences of those non-governmental organisations (NGOs) that have interacted with the AU.

There are good reasons for engaging with the AU. It is the premier inter-governmental organisation for the African continent. It is the body responsible for the realisation of African unity and political and economic integration, and for promoting Africa's social, political, economic and cultural development. It is the principal organisation for promoting Africa's relations with the outside world, its image and the interests of its citizens.

Non-African governments and multilateral agencies recognise the strategic role played by the AU. Among those who have appointed special representatives to the AU are the United States of America, China, India, the United Nations (UN) and the European Union (EU). They also send representatives to AU Summits and other AU meetings.

There are important proposals under discussion for the restructuring of the AU and its organs, to advance the integration of the African continent more rapidly. These discussions create new opportunities for interaction between civil society and AU organs.

This guide aims to help those organisations that wish to engage the AU but do not currently know where to start by providing an outline of the key institutions and processes and suggesting ways to influence them.

The Guide is divided into three sections:

> Part 1: A description of AU organs and institutions.
> Part 2: Suggestions on how to influence AU decisions and policy processes.
> Part 3: A summary of the debate to restructure the AU into a 'Union Government'.

Part One
AU Organs & Institutions

> Assembly of Heads of State and Government

> Chairperson of the African Union

> Executive Council of Ministers

> Permanent Representatives Committee (PRC)

> Commission of the African Union

> Peace and Security Council (PSC)

> Pan-African Parliament (PAP)

> African Commission on Human and Peoples' Rights (ACHPR)

> African Committee of Experts on the Rights and Welfare of the Child

> African Court on Human and Peoples' Rights (to become the African Court of Justice and Human Rights)

> Economic, Social and Cultural Council (ECOSOCC)

> New Partnership for Africa's Development (NEPAD)

> African Peer Review Mechanism (APRM)

> Specialised Technical Committees (STCs)

> Financial Institutions

> Funding of the African Union

> Regional Economic Communities (RECs)

The African Union is the successor to the Organisation of African Unity (OAU), the inter-governmental organisation for African states in existence since 1963, created with the aim of strengthening integration among Member States and the voice of the African continent in global affairs.

With the end of the Cold War, the final liberation of South Africa, and the reshaping of the international political scene, African Heads of State recognised that the OAU framework was no longer adequate to meet the needs for greater continental policy coordination and stronger economic growth, and that a greater commitment to democratic government at national level was necessary to strengthen Africa's own voice on the international stage. The structures of the European Union were taken as a model for a new configuration of the African continental body.

The Constitutive Act of the AU, its founding document, was adopted by Heads of State in 2000 in Lomé, Togo, and entered into force in 2001. The inaugural summit of the AU was held in Durban, South Africa, in July 2002. Its first objective is to 'Achieve greater unity and solidarity among African countries and among the peoples of Africa'.

Whereas the purposes set out in the OAU Charter focused on the defence of the sovereignty, territorial integrity and independence of African states and the eradication of all forms of colonialism from Africa, the AU has a much broader set of objectives, including the promotion of peace, security, and stability; democratic principles and institutions, popular participation and good governance; and human and peoples' rights.

The AU has 53 Member States. Only Morocco is not a member among states on the continent; it withdrew from the OAU in 1984 to protest the admission of the Sahrawi Arab Democratic Republic (Western Sahara) as a member.

Embedded within the structures of the AU is the African Economic Community (AEC), established by a treaty adopted in Abuja, Nigeria, in 1991, 'as an integral part of the OAU', and sharing a secretariat with OAU (now AU) structures. The Constitutive Act of the AU and the Abuja Treaty of the AEC are complementary and jointly provide the legal bases for continental integration.

Most of the key organs of the AU are established under the provisions of the AU Constitutive Act. But some are set up under protocols to the Constitutive Act or to the Abuja Treaty establishing the AEC, free-standing treaties or other legal documentation. The rest of Part 1 describes these bodies as they now exist. Important reforms are planned to these structures, discussed in Part 3.

4

STRUCTURES OF THE AFRICAN UNION

Organs established or proposed under the Constitutive Act:

> Assembly of Heads of State and Government (and its Chairperson)
> Executive Council of Ministers
> Permanent Representatives Committee
> Commission of the African Union
> Economic, Social and Cultural Council
> Pan-African Parliament
> Court of Justice
> Specialised Technical Committees
> Financial institutions: African Central Bank, African Investment Bank and African Monetary Fund.

Institutions and initiatives established by other treaties, protocols or agreements:

> Peace and Security Council
> African Commission on Human and Peoples' Rights
> African Committee of Experts on the Rights and Welfare of the Child
> African Court on Human and Peoples' Rights
> New Partnership for Africa's Development (NEPAD)
> African Peer Review Mechanism

Related institutions:

> Regional Economic Communities

> Assembly of Heads of State and Government

The Assembly of the African Union comprises the Heads of State and Government of all Member States and is the highest decision-making body of the AU. Since 2005, the Assembly has met in ordinary session twice (previously it was only once) a year, in January–February and in June–July. The Chairperson of the AU or any Member State can call an extraordinary session with the consent of at least two-thirds of all Member States.

The powers and functions of the Assembly are stipulated in Article 9 of the AU Constitutive Act and include the following:

> > Determination of the common policies of the Union
> > Monitoring the implementation of the decisions of the Union and ensuring compliance by Member States
> > Issue of directives and regulations to the Executive Council
> > Oversight over the affairs of the Union
> > Establishment of new organs of the Union
> > Appointment of certain categories of the AU personnel according to their respective rules and procedures
> > Consideration of requests for membership of the Union
> > Approval and adoption of the AU budget

The Assembly adopts decisions by majority vote. At most summits, the Assembly will adopt two types of proposal: *decisions*, which are binding on Member States according to their language; and *declarations*, which are intended to guide and harmonise the viewpoints of Member States but are not binding. Voting is by secret ballot, except for election of the Chairperson and Deputy-Chairpersons.

Treaties (Conventions and Charters) and their Protocols are adopted by decision but enter into force only after they have been ratified by a sufficient number of Member States, and legally bind those Member States that have ratified them.

For a list of African Heads of State visit:
www.africa-union.org/root/au/memberstates/Heads_of_State_and_Government.htm

If any Member State fails to comply with the decisions and policies of the AU, the Assembly can impose sanctions under Article 23 of the Constitutive Act, including not only denial of the right to speak and vote at meetings, but also 'measures of a political and economic nature' such as the denial of transport and communication links with other Member States.

> Chairperson of the African Union

A Head of State is elected by the Assembly to serve a one-year term as Chairperson of the AU. The Chairperson of the AU chairs meetings of the Assembly and guides the proceedings. Between sessions, he or she represents the AU both within Africa and on the international stage, and may assist in conflict resolution initiatives or other matters. There is not, however, a clear mechanism for ensuring that the views expressed by the Chairperson reflect a consensus of all Member States.

The Head of State who is Chairperson of the AU chairs the Assembly of Heads of State and Government. The Minister of Foreign Affairs of the same Member State chairs the Executive Council and the Ambassador to the AU chairs the Permanent Representatives Committee. The Chairperson's State is usually (though not always) the host of the mid-year summit.

The choice of Chairperson for the AU has already caused controversy. In 2005, Sudan began lobbying to be elected the next Chairperson of the African Union at the July summit, taking over from President Obasanjo of Nigeria. Because of concerns over the conflict in Sudan's Darfur Province, Obasanjo's AU term was instead extended by six months. In January 2006, Sudan was rebuffed once again, even though the summit was held in Khartoum rather than Addis Ababa as is usual for the January meetings. President Sassou Nguesso of the Republic of Congo took the seat instead and the Assembly also decided to create a Committee 'to consider the implementation of a rotation system between the regions' in relation to the presidency. In January 2007, Sudan again lost out to President Kufuor of Ghana (celebrating 50 years of independence that year); and in January 2008, when the East African region (of which Sudan forms part) finally got its turn, the presidency went instead to Tanzania.

Chairpersons of the African Union since it was founded:	
July 2002 – July 2003	Thabo Mbeki, South Africa
July 2003 – July 2004	Joaquim Chissano, Mozambique
July 2004 – Dec 2005	Olusegun Obasanjo, Nigeria (term extended by 6 months)
Jan – Dec 2006	Denis Sassou Nguesso, Republic of Congo
Jan – Dec 2007	John Agyekum Kufuor, Ghana
Jan – Dec 2008	Jakaya Kikwete, Tanzania
Jan – Dec 2009	Muammar Al-Gaddafi, Libya

NGO Action: The Darfur Consortium

The conflict in Darfur, Sudan, has claimed the lives of more than 250 000 people and displaced more than a million. The Darfur Consortium is a coalition of more than thirty NGOs committed to end the ongoing humanitarian and human rights crisis. The Consortium was formed on the fringes of the third extraordinary session of the African Commission on Human and Peoples' Rights, which was called to discuss the situation in Sudan and was held in Pretoria, South Africa in 2004.

The Consortium has ensured that the Darfur crisis has been on the agenda of AU summits since it began. This work has included engagement not just with political organs of the AU, such as the summit of Heads of State, but also with individual leading states and continental rights bodies such as the African Commission on Human and Peoples' Rights.

In particular, the Consortium opposed Sudan's bid to take over the chair of the AU from Nigeria, as representative of the East African region. The Consortium mobilised both its own members and a wider group of civil society organisations to sign strong statements opposing Sudan's candidacy in advance of the January 2006 Khartoum summit, where Sudan fully expected to be elected by the Assembly. Individual Consortium members lobbied hard in their own countries. A letter from the outgoing AU Chairman, President Olusegun Obasanjo of Nigeria, indicated that the issues raised by the Consortium were fundamental and that they would be considered at the summit. Sudanese security agents' disruption of a Consortium workshop held in Khartoum (despite visa difficulties) on justice and accountability issues in Africa, including Darfur, received extensive media coverage and diplomatic condemnation. The Assembly decided to appoint President Denis Sassou-Nguesso of the Republic of Congo as Chairperson of the AU in place of Sudan.

Sudan was a candidate for the Chairperson once again in January 2007. Consortium partners distributed flyers, organised demonstrations, a prayer service and other events for Darfur at the World Social Forum held in Nairobi in early December 2006, in addition to collecting 500 signatures from participants for a solidarity petition to the leaders of the AU. At the January 2007 Addis Ababa summit, Heads of State decided to extend the Chairperson of the African Union to Ghana, in honour of the 50th anniversary of its independence.

Darfur Consortium: www.darfurconsortium.org

> Executive Council of Ministers

The Executive Council is composed of Ministers of Foreign Affairs. It takes some decisions in its own right, and also prepares decisions for and reports to the Assembly.

The Executive Council has powers under the Constitutive Act to coordinate and take decisions in the areas of foreign trade, energy, industry and mineral resources, food security, agriculture and animal resources, livestock production and forestry, water resources and irrigation, environmental protection, humanitarian action and disaster response and relief, transport and communications, insurance, education, culture, health and human resources development.

The Executive Council is also responsible for administrative and legal matters, including the elections of AU officials, as delegated by the Assembly. Since 2003, it has been delegated by the Assembly to debate and approve the activity reports of the African Commission on Human and Peoples' Rights and the African Court on Human and Peoples' Rights, before they are published.

The AU regions and the Bureau

In addition to plenary meetings of AU organs attended by all Member States, many important decisions are taken among sub-groups of Member States, in particular at the level of the five political regions of the AU, and by the members of the bureau elected each year to manage the AU's affairs. While these meetings also take place at Head of State and Foreign Minister level, the discussions among representatives within the PRC are the most regular, carry out most of the preparatory work, and manage day-to-day business.

The five regions of the AU – Member States of the AU are divided into five geographic regions – east, west, north, southern and central Africa (see Appendix 1 for a map indicating the five regions). Each regional caucus elects a 'dean' each year who convenes meetings to determine common positions on key issues. These are separate consultations from those at the level of the Regional Economic Communities (see below), though the overlapping membership means that positions may coincide.

The Member States of the five regions of the AU are as follows:

EAST
Comoros, Djibouti, Ethiopia, Eritrea, Kenya, Madagascar, Mauritius, Rwanda, Somalia, Seychelles, Sudan, Tanzania, Uganda.

CENTRAL
Burundi, Cameroon, Central African Republic, Chad, Democratic Republic of Congo, Republic of Congo, Equatorial Guinea, Gabon, São Tomé and Príncipe.

NORTH
Algeria, Egypt, Libya, Mauritania, Sahrawi Arab Democratic Republic, Tunisia.

SOUTH
Angola, Botswana, Lesotho, Malawi, Mozambique, Namibia, South Africa, Swaziland, Zambia, Zimbabwe.

WEST
Benin, Burkina Faso, Cabo Verde, Côte d'Ivoire, Gambia, Ghana, Guinea-Bissau, Guinea, Liberia, Mali, Nigeria, Niger, Senegal, Sierra Leone, Togo.

The bureau – Each year at the mid-year summit, a bureau of 15 Member States (three from each region) is elected to guide the AU processes for the next year. The bureau at PRC level is responsible for preparations for summits, including determining the provisional agenda. The bureau meets as a drafting committee for key decisions and discusses strategies on how to handle sensitive issues.

> Permanent Representatives Committee (PRC)

The Permanent Representatives Committee (PRC) is made up of all the ambassador-level representatives of Member States accredited to the AU in Addis Ababa. The PRC has oversight of the day-to-day running of the Commission, making it one of the most influential organs of the AU. It meets at least once a month, usually at the AU headquarters in Addis Ababa.

The PRC is mandated by the Constitutive Act to work closely with the Commission to implement AU programmes and to monitor the implementation of decisions reached at summits. According to the PRC's rules of procedure, any Member State, AU organ or Regional Economic Community may propose items for the agenda.

Its powers and functions fall in four areas:
> Liaison between Member States and the AU Commission
> Oversight over the Commission
> Support to the Executive Council in executing its powers and functions
> Assisting the preparation of the Union's programme of activities

The PRC is supposed to meet at least once a month (usually in Addis Ababa) to discuss recommendations for adoption by the Executive Council.

The Constitutive Act and the Committee's rules of procedure allow it to form sub-committees to facilitate its work.

SUB-COMMITTEES OF THE PRC

The sub-committees discuss technical and administrative questions, as delegated by the full PRC.

> Advisory sub-committee on administrative, budgetary and financial matters
> Sub-committee on programmes and conferences
> Sub-committee on refugees
> Sub-committee on contributions
> Policy sub-committee of the Special Emergency Assistance Fund for drought and famine in Africa
> Sub-committee on structural reforms
> Sub-committee on headquarters and host agreements
> Sub-committee on economic and trade matters
> Sub-committee on multilateral cooperation

Commission of the African Union

> The African Union, and particularly its Commission, is ready to engage with civil society. You have immense contributions to make.
> — Ambassador John K. Shinkaiye,
>   Chief of Staff,
>   African Union Commission

The Commission of the African Union acts as the AU's secretariat and is based in Addis Ababa. According to the Constitutive Act, the Commission is composed of a Chairperson, his/her deputy or deputies, Commissioners and staff.

The Assembly determines the Commission's structure, functions and regulations and elects the Chairperson and Deputy Chairperson; the other commissioners are elected by the Council of Ministers and appointed by the Assembly. There are eight Commissioners, who manage the day-today tasks of the AU in relation to their portfolios. These officials hold office for concurrent four-year terms.

The Chairperson of the AU Commission reports to the Executive Council of Ministers.

In February 2009, the AU Assembly resolved to transform the AU Commission into an AU Authority, with stronger powers (discussed in Part 3). The responsibilities of the Commissioners will be slightly modified as part of this transformation: however, the basic structure of Chairperson, Deputy Chairperson and eight Commissioners (to be renamed Secretaries) remains. In the table below, the portfolio name is given both for the AU Commission and the new name under the AU Authority (if relevant). The list of responsibilities is based on the new assignments.

The Commission both initiates policy and budget proposals for consideration by other AU organs and is responsible for implementing the decisions of the PRC, Executive Council of Ministers and Assembly. It also provides operational support to the Peace and Security Council, ECOSOCC, the Committee of Experts on the Rights and Welfare of the Child and other AU activities.

As at late 2008, there were close to 700 people working for the AU Commission: though the approved complement is substantially larger the budget has not allowed more to be employed.

The African Citizens' and Diaspora Directorate (CIDO), located in the office of the chairperson, is the official liaison office for civil society organisations from Africa or the African diaspora wishing to interact with the Commission. CIDO is responsible for accrediting NGOs to attend summits and other meetings and acts also as the secretariat for ECOSOCC, the AU's civil society organ.

Responsibilities of the different Departments and Directorates within the AU Commission:

> OFFICE OF THE CHAIRPERSON

Office of the Legal Counsel
Status of country ratifications, drafting and interpretation of treaties

Women, Gender and Development Directorate
Gender issues, country reports for implementation of solemn declaration on women's rights

African Citizens' and Diaspora Directorate (CIDO)
Civil society and diaspora issues, accreditation to meetings, observer status, support to ECOSOCC

> OFFICE OF THE DEPUTY CHAIRPERSON

Conferences and Events
Organisation of AU meetings

Human resources
Management of AU Commission staff

Finance and budget
Analysis of AU budget and resource allocation priorities

Protocol
Accreditation procedures

> DEPARTMENTS HEADED BY COMMISSIONERS

Peace and Security
New name: Peace Security and Common Defence
> Conflict prevention and management, peacekeeping, terrorism, transnational crime

Political Affairs
New name: Political Affairs and Coordination of Common Positions on External Relations
> Political cooperation, governance, elections, human rights, humanitarian affairs, free movement of persons, financial crimes

Infrastructure and Energy
> Transport and energy infrastructure

Social Affairs
New Name: Health and Social Affairs
> Children, crime prevention, human trafficking, population, migration, labour and employment, sports and culture, epidemics including HIV and AIDS

Human Resources, Science and Technology
New Name: Education, Human Resources and Science and Technology
> Information and communication technology, youth, research, universities, intellectual property

Trade and Industry
New name: Trade, Industry and International Cooperation
> International trade negotiations, trade, industry, customs and immigration, free movement of goods and services, tourism

Rural Economy and Agriculture
New name: Rural Economy, Agriculture and Environment
> Agriculture and food security, livestock, water, desertification, natural resources, climate change

Economic Affairs
> Economic integration, international economic cooperation, monetary affairs, private sector development, investment and resource mobilisation, poverty reduction, statistics

NGO Action: Women's rights coalitions work with the AU Commission

In 2003, after a long campaign by women's rights groups, the Assembly approved a Protocol to the African Charter on Human and Peoples' Rights on the Rights of Women in Africa. It is one of the most far-sighted instruments on women's rights anywhere in the world. By July 2004, only Comoros had ratified the Protocol. Women's rights organisations – including the coalition Solidarity for African Women's Rights (SOAWR), the African Women's Development and Communication Network (FEMNET), WILDAF-West Africa and Southern Africa Women's Agenda – found an enthusiastic partner in the AU Commission's Women, Gender and Development Directorate for advocacy to achieve ratification by 15 countries, the minimum number required before the protocol could enter into force.

The SOAWR coalition reached out to national women's organisations and formed a Pan-African steering committee with Equality Now in Kenya as its secretariat. It published books, issued press releases and lobbied AU staff and permanent representatives, as well as submitting a petition to Heads of State for the ratification of the Protocol on the Rights of Women and issuing 'report cards' at summits on whether Member States had yet ratified.

Femmes Africa Solidarité (FAS) also worked with the AU Commission's Women, Gender and Development Directorate to lobby successfully for the creation of an African Women's Committee for Peace and Development and has collaborated with the Commission and the new Committee in the 'Gender Is My Agenda' campaign on violence against women.

At the July 2004 summit in Addis Ababa, the Assembly adopted the Solemn Declaration on Gender Equality in Africa, committing the AU to gender parity in its appointments, and African leaders to action to address a range of issues affecting gender equality, including the impact of HIV and AIDS on women.

The Protocol on the Rights of Women in Africa received its fifteenth ratification and entered into force in November 2005, less than two years after women's organisations began their campaign for national ratifications.

SOAWR: www.soawr.org
FEMNET: www.femnet.or.ke
FAS: www.fasngo.org
WILDAF: www.wildaf.org.zw
Gender is my Agenda Campaign: www.genderismyagenda.com

> Peace and Security Council (PSC)

The Peace and Security Council (PSC) was established as an organ of the AU under a protocol to the Constitutive Act adopted by the AU Assembly in July 2002. The protocol defines the PSC as a collective security and early warning arrangement to facilitate timely and effective response to conflict and crisis situations in Africa.

The PSC has the power, among other things, to authorise peace support missions, to impose sanctions in case of unconstitutional change of government, and to 'take initiatives and action it deems appropriate' in response to potential or actual conflicts. The PSC is a decision-making body in its own right, and its decisions are binding on Member States.

Article 4 of the Constitutive Act, repeated in article 4 of the PSC Protocol, recognises the right of the Union to intervene in a Member State in case of war crimes, genocide and crimes against humanity. Any decision to intervene in a Member State under article 4 of the Constitutive Act will be made by the Assembly on the recommendation of the PSC.

The Peace and Security Council is also responsible for implementation of the Non-aggression and Common Defence Pact adopted in 2005, among whose commitments are that 'State Parties undertake to prohibit and prevent genocide, other forms of mass murder as well as crimes against humanity'.

The PSC comprises 15 Member States with equal voting rights elected by the Assembly for two- or three-year terms.

The Council operates at three levels:

> Heads of state – must meet at least once a year
> Ministerial representatives – must meet at least once a year
> Permanent representatives – must meet twice a month and more often if required

The Chairperson of the Council can call a meeting at any time.

Since it first met in 2004, the PSC has been active in relation to the crises in Darfur, Comoros, Somalia, Democratic Republic of Congo, Burundi, Côte d'Ivoire and other countries. It has recommended the creation of AU peacekeeping operations in Somalia and Darfur, and the imposition of sanctions against persons undermining peace and security (such as travel bans and asset freezes imposed in 2007 against the leaders of a rebellion in Comoros). The Council is overseeing the establishment of the AU Standby Force which will serve as a permanent African security force. There are proposals to involve the PSC in the enforcement of the decisions of the African Commission on Human and Peoples' Rights.

Article 20 of the PSC protocol requires the PSC to encourage civil society organisations 'to participate actively in the efforts aimed at promoting peace, security and stability in Africa' and allows the PSC to invite them to address it directly. In December 2008, the PSC adopted a document setting out the modalities for interaction with civil society organisations, known as the 'Livingstone Formula'. The formula provides for the PSC to consult with ECOSOCC and invite individual civil society organisations to address its meetings. Civil society organisations from both Kenya and Zimbabwe have briefed members of the PSC on events in their countries, and South Africa's Institute for Security Studies has formally briefed the PSC itself.

The PSC Secretariat is based in the Peace and Security Department at the AU Commission headquarters in Addis Ababa.

PSC documents available by searching the AU website:
www.africa-union.org

Institute for Security Studies website on African organisations, with links to the AU and PSC documents:
www.issafrica.org/organisations.php

NGO Action: SaferAfrica and SalaamNet

SaferAfrica, a South African NGO, provided support to the AU Commission's Peace and Security Department which led to the Executive Council's adoption of a policy on post-conflict reconstruction and development at the June 2006 summit in Banjul, Gambia. SaferAfrica led the team that drafted the policy framework after several experts' meetings on peacekeeping, reconstruction and stability. SaferAfrica will provide a pool of technical experts to support implementation at regional and national levels.

SaferAfrica: www.saferafrica.org/progs/peace/pcrd.php

SalaamNet was formed in November 2006 as a network to provide the AU and its partners with detailed research and analysis to inform conflict resolution and prevention. Composed largely of NGOs, with a secretariat based at the Institute for Security Studies (South Africa) office in Addis Ababa, SalaamNet aims to enhance the capacity of African civil society and the continental institutions to produce high quality research on conflict issues, and to play a complementary role to other continental structures, including ECOSOCC and the RECs, as well as the Peace and Security Council.

Salaamnet: www.salaamnet.org

> Pan-African Parliament (PAP)

The Pan-African Parliament (PAP) is recognised as one of the organs of the AU under the Constitutive Act, though its detailed legal basis is a protocol to the 1991 Abuja Treaty establishing the African Economic Community. The PAP has its secretariat in Midrand, South Africa, where it holds its regular sessions in November and March each year. It first met in March 2004.

According to the protocol, PAP is expected to exercise advisory and consultative functions. These functions are to be reviewed after five years of its existence, with a view to giving it stronger powers, including to pass legislation. In January 2009, the Assembly authorised the AU Commission to initiate this review process. PAP reports to the Assembly and its budget is processed through the policy organs of the AU. It is presided over by a Bureau headed by a Chairperson and four Vice Chairpersons. It has ten permanent committees responsible for different thematic issues and the management of the parliament's business.

Each of the Member States that have ratified the PAP is entitled to five representatives to its meetings, selected from national parliaments or other deliberative bodies, at least one of whom must be a woman. As of August 2009, all AU Member States except Côte d'Ivoire, the Democratic Republic of Congo, Eritrea, Guinea, Somalia, and São Tomé and Príncipe had ratified the PAP protocol.

> African Commission on Human and Peoples' Rights (ACHPR)

The African Commission on Human and Peoples' Rights (ACHPR) was established in 1986 in accordance with the provisions of the African Charter on Human and Peoples' Rights, and works to protect and promote the rights set out in the Charter. Its secretariat is located in Banjul, Gambia. The 11 Commissioners, who are nominated by Member States but serve in their personal capacity, meet in ordinary session twice a year. The Commission can also call extraordinary sessions, and did so in 1995 following the execution of Ken Saro-Wiwa in Nigeria, and in 2004 in response to the crisis in Darfur (as well as on other occasions for more procedural matters).

States are supposed to report to the Commission every two years on the measures they have taken to give effect to the rights in the Charter, but many are in default of this obligation.

African and international human rights organisations can obtain observer status with the African Commission. Once they have observer status, they can submit documentation and speak at the Commission's sessions. An NGO forum is also usually organised in advance of each African Commission session. NGOs are very often co-opted by the Commission to contribute to the work of its special mechanisms (special rapporteurs and working groups) or to help in organising seminars. Many of the important documents adopted by the Commission have been drafted with the assistance of human rights NGOs. Individuals, or organisations on their behalf, can lodge complaints with the Commission of violations by Member States of the African Charter on Human and Peoples' Rights. Since it first met, the Commission has ruled against Member States on a wide range of issues.

The Commission reports to the Executive Council at each summit, and its decisions on individual complaints are not public until they have been adopted by the Council and Assembly.

African Commission on Human and Peoples' Rights:
www.achpr.org

NGO Action: NGOs working with the African human rights institutions

The Institute for Human Rights and Development in Africa and the African Centre for Democracy and Human Rights Studies are both NGOs based in Banjul, close to the secretariat of the African Commission on Human and Peoples' Rights, and work to facilitate civil society engagement with the ACHPR and other African human rights bodies.

The African Centre has for many years hosted NGO forums in advance of the sessions of the Commission; while the Institute has conducted trainings on the African human rights system for African human rights activists, worked with the Commission and with the African Committee of Experts on the Rights and Welfare of the Child on the drafting of their procedures, and has also brought individual communications to the Commission and Committee of Experts.

Institute for Human Rights and Development in Africa: www.africaninstitute.org
African Centre for Democracy and Human Rights Studies: www.acdhrs.org

> African Committee of Experts on the Rights and Welfare of the Child

The African Committee of Experts on the Rights and Welfare of the Child was established in 2001, with the mandate to protect and promote the rights set out in the African Charter on the Rights and Welfare of the Child (adopted in 1990, entered into force 1999). It usually meets twice a year to consider reports from member governments on the implementation of the Charter. It then drafts a report to be tabled before the Assembly of Heads of State and Government. The Committee of Experts has a small secretariat in Addis Ababa, based at the AU Commission.

African Court on Human and Peoples' Rights (to become the African Court of Justice and Human Rights)

A 1998 protocol to the African Charter on Human and Peoples' Rights to establish an African Court on Human and Peoples' Rights came into force in 2004. The first judges were sworn in during the July 2006 AU summit, and the Court is based in Arusha, Tanzania.

In addition, the Constitutive Act provides for a Court of Justice to rule on disputes over interpretation of AU treaties. A protocol to set up the Court of Justice was adopted in 2003, but did not enter into force.

A decision to merge the two courts and establish a combined African Court of Justice and Human Rights was taken at the June 2004 summit. In July 2008, Heads of State finally adopted the Protocol on the Statute of the African Court of Justice and Human Rights, which will supersede the two existing protocols. The merged court, which will also be based in Arusha, will have two chambers, for human rights and general matters. The new protocol will come into effect once 15 states have ratified it; in the meantime the African Court on Human and Peoples' Rights remains in place.

The Court of Justice and Human Rights will have the authority to judge disputes about the Constitutive Act and the other protocols and treaties adopted by the AU (or the OAU), including the African Charter on Human and Peoples' Rights and its protocols. The rules for accessing the courts are slightly different; however, individuals and NGOs do not have the right to refer either to the existing court or the merged court unless a State Party has made a specific declaration allowing them to do so in human rights cases, as provided under both the relevant protocols. Cases will be able to be referred to the merged court by AU Member States that have ratified the protocol, by the Assembly, PAP and other organs of the AU authorised by the Assembly, or a staff member of the AU in relation to certain disputes; the Court will not have the jurisdiction to rule on disputes involving states that have not ratified the Protocol. Cases alleging violations of human rights instruments ratified by Member States can additionally be referred to the merged court by the African Commission on Human and Peoples' Rights; the African Committee of Experts on the Rights and Welfare of the Child; African intergovernmental organisations accredited to the AU or its organs; and African national human rights institutions.

In 2009, the AU decided to consider the possibility of empowering the Court to try persons accused of international crimes (crimes against humanity and war crimes).

AU treaties and their status:
www.africa-union.org/root/AU/Documents/Treaties/treaties.htm

NGO Action: Coalition for an Effective African Court

The Coalition for an Effective African Court on Human and Peoples' Rights, a network of NGOs and national human rights institutions, was formed during the first conference for the promotion of the Protocol to the African Charter on Human and Peoples' Rights establishing the African Court in Niamey, Niger in May 2003. It has an office in Arusha, Tanzania.

The key purpose for its establishment is to have an effective and independent African Court on Human and Peoples' Rights in order to provide redress to victims of human rights violations and strengthen the human rights protection system in African and at domestic level.

The objectives of the Coalition include the ratification of the Protocol establishing the African Court on Human and Peoples' Rights by all AU Member States; enhance transparency in the nomination and election of judges; develop capacity for litigation and promote direct access by individuals to take cases to the Court directly.

The Coalition has contributed to the creation of the African Court of Justice and Human Rights to ensure that the merged court does not compromise the human rights element. A number of Member States have ratified the Protocol establishing the Court as a result of the Coalition's advocacy.

Coalition for an Effective African Court: www.africancourtcoalition.org

Economic, Social and Cultural Council (ECOSOCC)

ECOSOCC is an advisory organ designed to give civil society organisations (CSOs) a voice within the AU institutions and decision-making processes. It is provided for in the Constitutive Act, but does not have its own protocol, relying rather on Statutes approved by the Assembly that have a lesser legal status and can more easily be amended. ECOSOCC is made up of civil society organisations from a wide range of sectors including labour, business and professional groups, service providers and policy think tanks, both from within Africa and the African diaspora.

The ECOSOCC Statutes provide for four main bodies:

> A 150-member General Assembly, made up of 144 elected representatives (two from each Member State, ten operating at regional level, eight at continental level and 20 from the diaspora) and six representatives of CSOs nominated by the AU Commission, to be the highest decision-making body of the organ.
> A 15-member standing committee with representatives from the five regions of Africa to coordinate the work of the organ.
> Ten sectoral cluster committees for feeding opinion and inputs into the policies and programmes of the AU.
> A five-person credentials committee for determining the eligibility of CSO representatives to contest elections or participate in the processes of the organ.

The criteria established by the ECOSOCC Statutes for membership include that candidates should:

> Be national, regional, continental or African diaspora CSOs, without restriction to undertake regional or international activities.
> Have objectives and principles that are consistent with the principles and objectives of the Union.
> Be registered in a Member State of the African Union and/or meet the general conditions of eligibility for the granting of observer status to non-governmental organisations.

> Show proof that the ownership and management of the CSO is made up of not less than 50 per cent of Africans or African diaspora.

> Show that the resources of the organisation derive at least 50 per cent from contributions of the members of the organisation.

The requirements on funding from membership contributions mean that many African NGOs are not eligible for membership of ECOSOCC.

Interim ECOSOCC structures were established in 2005, under the leadership of Interim Chairperson Wangari Maathai of Kenya. Elections to the ECOSOCC structures were finally held in 23 African states and at continental level in late 2007. The eight members of the ECOSOCC Assembly at continental level are the Pan-African Lawyers Union (PALU), the Organisation of African Trade Union Unity (OATUU), the Pan-African Employers Federation, the Africa IDP Voice, the Network of African Peace Builders, and women's groups FEMNET, the Pan-African Women's Organisation (PAWO) and Femmes Africa Solidarité (FAS).

Although elections had not been completed, the official launch of the new ECOSOCC General Assembly took place in Dar es Salaam, Tanzania, on 9 September 2008, under the presidency of Cameroonian lawyer Akere Muna. The Assembly decided to resume the election process and invited nominations for election to the Assembly from the countries that had not yet chosen members. In December 2008, the ECOSOCC Assembly held a meeting in Abuja, Nigeria, to discuss a strategic plan for the organ and begin a review of the ECOSOCC Statutes.

The CIDO office in the AU Commission acts as secretariat for ECOSOCC.

ECOSOCC officers have the potential to be a critical link for civil society to the AU. As full delegates to the AU summits, they can attend all meetings, including closed sessions, and are in a position to brief CSOs on key issues tabled. ECOSOCC is required to submit a report on its activities to the AU Assembly.

Websites for **ECOSOCC and CIDO:**
www.africa-union.org/ECOSOCC/CIDO-en.htm
www.africa-union.org/root/AU/AUC/Departments/BCP/CIDO/cido.htm

New Partnership for Africa's Development (NEPAD)

NEPAD is a programme for Africa's economic development that was first adopted in 2001 outside the structures of the OAU/AU. It was endorsed by the first AU summit in Durban in 2002. The NEPAD founding document champions good governance as a basic requirement for peace, security and sustainable political and socio-economic development.

The NEPAD secretariat reports to the NEPAD Heads of State and Government Implementation Committee (HSGIC), which usually meets in the margins of AU summits and in turn reports to the Assembly. The NEPAD Secretariat is based in Midrand, South Africa. Its activities are funded by voluntary contributions from Member States.

The initial plan of NEPAD adopts a three-pronged strategy for action: establishing preconditions for sustainable development (including peace and security and improved governance); identifying priority sectors for action (education, health, regional infrastructure, agriculture, market access, and the environment); and mobilising resources to achieve NEPAD's aims.

The NEPAD Secretariat works with the RECs, which are primarily responsible for implementing the NEPAD programmes, to promote effective cross-border collaboration on infrastructure, trade and other economic initiatives. Among the NEPAD flagship projects is the Comprehensive Africa Agriculture Development Programme (CAADP).

The extent of civil society participation in NEPAD programmes is largely dependent on the capacity of civil society groups. A civil society desk at the NEPAD Secretariat provides a one-stop focal point. All programmes are implemented in consultation with the relevant civil society groups.

— Prof. Wiseman L. Nkuhlu, former chief executive, NEPAD

NEPAD:
www.nepad.org

NGO Action: The African Trade Network and the Global Call to Action Against Poverty (GCAP)

Established in 1998, the Africa Trade Network (ATN) has 25 members from 15 countries across Africa. The network has built a constituency to monitoring and influence assertive common African positions in negotiations with the World Trade Organisation and the European Union's Economic Partnership Agreements. The ATN has observer status with the African Union, and has provided a means of increased interaction between civil society groups and African governments, including at the annual Conference of African Ministers of Trade.

Africa Trade Network Secretariat (at Third World Network, Ghana): www.twnafrica.org

The Global Call to Action Against Poverty is an international coalition formed in 2003 that seeks debt cancellation, fair trade terms and a substantial aid increase to all countries that have a budgetary shortfall for realising the Millennium Development Goals (MDGs). A Pan-African steering committee works with affiliates in 33 African countries. GCAP organisers attended the January 2005 AU summit and lobbied policy makers. In March that year they participated in an AU experts' meeting on debt and submitted a memorandum to the NEPAD Secretariat before the G8 meeting in July 2005 that had Africa as a principal focus. On the international front, GCAP members attended the July G8 Heads of State meeting, the September UN Millennium Review Summit and the December World Trade Organisation inter-ministerial conference. GCAP affiliates remain active on the continent, engaging with the regional economic communities, such as ECOWAS, and demanding action from the AU summits on poverty, access to education and health care, and action against the government of Zimbabwe for human rights violations and failure to respect elections.

GCAP: www.whiteband.org

> African Peer Review Mechanism (APRM)

The African Peer Review Mechanism (APRM) is a self-monitoring mechanism by which Member States of the AU can agree to independent review of their fulfilment of the governance commitments contained in African and international standards. Initially established as part of the NEPAD initiative, the APRM now operates independently under a Memorandum of Understanding signed by Member States on a voluntary basis.

Signatories agree to conduct their own national self-assessments of compliance with a range of African and international governance standards. These self-assessments are supposed to be prepared through a highly participatory research process that generates a 'national conversation' about governance challenges. They are reviewed by a Panel of Eminent Persons who prepare their own independent report, which is presented to a meeting of all the Heads of State and Government who have signed the APRM memorandum (known as the APR Forum). The report is then discussed with the Head of State whose country is being reviewed. Each review leads to a National Programme of Action to address the problems identified. States report each year on their progress in implementing the Programme of Action to the APR Forum.

As of August 2009, 30 countries had voluntarily acceded to the mechanism. Among them, 12 countries had completed their reviews (Algeria, Benin, Burkina Faso, Ghana, Lesotho, Kenya, Mali, Mozambique, Nigeria, Rwanda, South Africa and Uganda).

Member states of the APRM (August 2009)

Algeria, Angola, Benin, Burkina Faso, Cameroon, Cape Verde, Republic of Congo, Djibouti, Egypt, Ethiopia, Gabon, Ghana, Kenya, Lesotho, Malawi, Mali, Mauritania, Mauritius, Mozambique, Nigeria, Rwanda, São Tome and Príncipe, Senegal, Sierra Leone, South Africa, Sudan, Tanzania, Togo, Uganda and Zambia.

The APRM Secretariat is located in Midrand, South Africa, close to the NEPAD Secretariat. It is largely funded by those Member States that have signed the APRM memorandum, with contributions from external donors. There is a great deal of scope for civil society participation in the APRM process at national level; but much less when it comes to the examination of the final report by Heads of State.

Official APRM website:
www.aprm-international.org

NGO Action: Advocacy with the APRM

AfriMAP, the Africa Governance Monitoring and Advocacy Project of the Open Society Institute's network of Africa foundations, has commissioned reviews of the APRM process in almost all the countries where it has taken place. Each report has focused on civil society involvement in the process of preparing the country self-assessment reports, and the extent to which these reports lived up to the participatory ideals of the APRM. The reports have been launched in each country, with recommendations on strengthening civil society engagement with the APRM and its follow-up processes; and also used in advocacy with the APRM Secretariat and Panel of Eminent Persons at continental level. AfriMAP has also worked with national civil society organisations on submissions to the APRM country review missions.

Other civil society organisations that follow the APRM closely and can provide background information include: the South African Institute of International Affairs (SAIIA), the Electoral Institute of Southern Africa (EISA) and Partnership Africa Canada (PAC). SAIIA's 2008 study *The African Peer Review Mechanism: Lessons from the Pioneers* provides a comprehensive analysis of the APRM process in the first countries to complete the reviews.

AfriMAP: www.afrimap.org
SAIIA: www.saiia.org.za
EISA: www.eisa.org.za
PAC: www.pacweb.org

> Specialised Technical Committees (STC)

Both the Abuja Treaty and the Constitutive Act provide for the creation of Specialised Technical Committees (STCs) made up of African ministers. The STCs are to prepare projects and programmes of the Union and submit them to the Executive Council, with the aim of reducing the number of ad hoc ministerial meetings. These STCs had not been created by the end of 2008, but in January 2009 the Assembly decided to reconfigure them into a set of 14 (rather than the seven proposed by the Constitutive Act), each with a thematic responsibility.

PART 1: AU ORGANS & INSTITUTIONS

33

> Financial Institutions

The Constitutive Act provides for the AU to have three financial institutions: an African Central Bank, African Monetary Fund; and African Investment Bank. These institutions are not yet in place, though discussions are underway with a view to establishing them. The Statutes of the African Investment Bank were formally adopted at the June 2009 AU summit and the Protocol establishing the bank opened for ratification by Member States.

> Funding of the African Union

There are three main sources of revenue for the AU. They are:

> Contributions by Member States according to a scale of assessment approved by the Executive Council
> Additional voluntary contributions by Member States to the solidarity fund
> Funds made available by external partners

Five of Africa's wealthiest Member States each contribute 15 per cent of the assessed contributions: Algeria, Egypt, Libya, Nigeria and South Africa. These states are particularly influential in AU decision-making. The remaining 25 per cent is paid by the other Member States.

The approved budget for the African Union for 2009 was US$ 164.3 million, to be split between Member State assessed contributions of $ 93.8 million, and development partners contributions of $ 57.4 million (and the remainder to be financed from previous budget surpluses).

The Chairperson of the Commission acts as chief accounting officer to the AU and submits the budget of the Union to the organs of the AU for approval. The budget is adopted by the Assembly on the recommendation of the Executive Council and after consideration by the PRC.

The AU can and does impose sanctions on countries that are in arrears with their subscriptions. These sanctions range from limited access to facilities to suspension of voting rights. It is common for several countries at one time not to have the right to vote at AU meetings because their dues are not paid; this suspension of voting rights also extends to that country's members of the Pan-African Parliament. Some countries in financial difficulty, such as those emerging from conflict, have successfully sought exemption from paying their subscriptions, or a reduction in the amount.

> Regional Economic Communities (RECs)

Both the 1980 Lagos Plan of Action for the Development of Africa and the 1991 Abuja Treaty to establish the African Economic Community proposed the creation of Regional Economic Communities (RECs) as the basis for African integration, with a timetable for regional and then continental integration to follow. There are eight RECs recognised by the AU, each established under a separate regional treaty. The membership of many of the communities overlaps, and their rationalisation has been under discussion for several years, and formed the theme of the 2006 Banjul summit. At the July 2007 Accra summit the Assembly adopted a Protocol on Relations between the African Union and the Regional Economic Communities. This protocol is intended to facilitate the harmonisation of policies and ensure compliance with the Abuja Treaty and Lagos Plan of Action time frames.

The RECs can be important fora for civil society activism both because of their importance in their own regions and because they have a voice in the discussions of the African Union. The Economic Community of West African States (ECOWAS) has the most formalised parallel civil society body, known as the West Africa Civil Society Forum (WACSOF).

Many of the RECs have their own courts, including ECOWAS, SADC and the EAC. Ordinary citizens and civil society organisations have the right to bring cases directly to these courts, and there have been important decisions from both the ECOWAS and SADC courts in favour of human rights principles. The East African Court of Justice has also ruled on issues relating to the composition of the East African Legislative Assembly.

The eight RECs recognised by the AU:
- The Arab Maghreb Union (UMA)
- The Common Market for Eastern and Southern Africa (COMESA)
- The Community of Sahel-Saharan States (CEN-SAD)
- The East African Community (EAC)
- The Economic Community of Central African States (ECCAS)
- The Economic Community of West African States (ECOWAS)
- The Intergovernmental Authority on Development (IGAD)
- The Southern Africa Development Community (SADC)

See Appendix 2 for a complete list of REC membership and objectives, and links to their websites.

Part Two

INFLUENCING
AU DECISIONS & POLICIES

Civil society organisations in Africa know the procedures of the UN, EU and even USAID, but they have not spent time learning about their own continental organisation, the African Union.

African NGOs rush to Geneva and New York for meetings. It's time they invested in the African Union. We must restructure our funding to allow for their participation in the African Union.

— Comments from civil society activists

The AU decision-making process

Decisions of the African Union Executive Council and Assembly are the result of work done months before each summit by the Commission and other organs, and in decision-making processes within individual member states. The majority of proposals presented to the Assembly have already been largely agreed before they are tabled at a summit.

Documents adopted by the Assembly usually start life as a policy proposal from one of the AU Commission's departments, from another AU organ or from a Member State. These proposals are debated in an experts' meeting, whose members are nominated by Member States, and then in a meeting called for the relevant Ministers from Member States to approve or amend the experts' proposals. With the exception of decisions with implications for the budget which are then considered by the PRC, the final documents from the ministerial meeting will go directly to the Executive Council and/ or Assembly for adoption.

> The PRC is reluctant to recommend proposals that have not gone through the expert group meeting. They are often sent back.
>
> — African Union official

Sometimes, this decision-making process is not followed exactly. This is the case when an item is urgently added to the AU summit agenda.

Tips on strategy: Entry points for civil society

- For every conference planned, there has been a planning committee.
- For every date agreed, there has been a larger calendar of events.
- For every paper presented, there has been a process for choosing issues and speakers.
- For every list of participants, there has been a discussion about who should attend.
- For every speech read out, there has been a speechwriter looking for ideas.

		THE AU POLICY CYCLE	
Stage	Forum	Description	NGO Action
1	**Member State or AU Commission proposal**	Proposals are introduced by Member States or a department or directorate of the AU Commission, or are referred to the Commission by the Executive Council	• Familiarise yourself with annual plans and summit decisions • Suggest proposals to Member States • Offer technical assistance and relevant information to draft documents • Organise brainstorming sessions
2	**Experts group meeting**	Most AU policy documents, treaties and programmes of action are scrutinised by a panel of experts appointed by the government and the AU Commission	• Seek invitations or nominate experts • Interact with individual experts • Offer to write short briefing papers • Facilitate meetings • Volunteer to draft reports • Brief ACHPR special rapporteurs
3	**Ministers meeting**	After the panel of experts, a proposal is submitted to a meeting of relevant sectoral ministers	• Seek invitation to be part of delegation or lobby in the meeting's margins • Brief ministers and officials while in home country • Share position papers • Talk to the press at national level what the proposal means
4	**PRC full meeting or subcommittee**	The PRC considers reports of ministerial meetings and determines items that should be on the agenda of the Executive Council	• Brief chair, members and regional caucuses • Offer suggestions on ways to fund the proposal • Give regular briefings on your issues to PRC members to establish credibility
5	**Executive Council**	The Executive Council reviews the recommendations from a ministerial meeting, and in some cases will make the final decision on a proposal	• Highlight negative consequences of not adopting proposal • Brief the press on importance of issues • Brief regional caucus meetings • Brief delegations and regional caucuses
6	**Assembly**	If approved by the Executive Council, and where necessary, a decision will be sent to the Assembly for final adoption	• If issue not decided, continue to gather support • If agreed, congratulate governments for taking bold and positive steps • Set up a monitoring mechanism

> Civil society engagement with the AU Organs

There are four main ways in which civil society organisations engage the AU:

1. **Institutional spaces**
   Members of ECOSOCC have an official place in AU structures
2. **Invited spaces**
   Any organisation may be invited to attend AU activities
3. **Created spaces**
   Organising autonomous activities related to AU issues and processes
4. **Joint spaces**
   Organising joint activities with AU organs

In addition to being members of the newly established ECOSOCC, NGOs may also apply for observer status with the AU (see below). Others have followed a different route and have signed memorandums of understanding with the AU Commission to provide technical assistance. Among these organisations are the International Institute for Democracy and Electoral Assistance (International IDEA), the European Centre for Development and Policy Management (ECDPM), and Oxfam.

Perhaps the most powerful initiatives, however, have been the independent advocacy efforts organised by civil society coalitions on particular policy issues (see the case studies throughout this Guide).

I don't mind civil society trying to influence our work – but for goodness sake, spell my name correctly!
— Ambassador and former chairperson, Permanent Representative Committee

Tips on strategy: Basic steps for civil society organisations seeking to lobby the AU

- Find out which countries are members of the bureau elected to guide AU processes during the year. Meet with them and present your arguments for your issue being on the agenda of the next summit... or the one after. Ask their advice on what would be needed for an agenda item to be agreed.

- Find out which country is the current dean of each regional group and the position of the region on critical issues. Meet with the ambassador of that country in Addis Ababa, together with representatives of NGOs from that region, present your viewpoint and find out where you stand.

- Make sure that you express your advocacy messages within the framework of AU policies and standards – and not only the international ones.

- Try to identify which countries are likely to wield the greatest influence for and against an issue of concern. Make contact with NGOs in those countries to strategise on ways to influence their positions.

- Where there are divided opinions among AU Member States, consider which countries might be able to broker a compromise, given their historical position, current influence or other factors. Meet with that country's ambassador and see what may be done.

- Find out what is the position of the five countries that together contribute 75 per cent of the AU budget. If members of the 'big five' budget contributors are hostile, seek to mobilise other countries who may have influence with them, or work even harder to create a critical mass of smaller countries whose opinion they will find hard to oppose.

- Put together a mapping of the positions taken by Member States and regions on important issues to help identify the most important countries to target and use to strategise with your allies.

- Establish and maintain cordial relations with staff of the AU Commission and diplomatic representatives of Member States based in Addis Ababa, or work with organisations which have established relations.

> NGO observer status with the AU

The July 2005 AU summit held in Sirte, Libya revised the criteria and procedures for granting observer status with the African Union to non-governmental organisations (NGOs).

NGOs seeking observer status must be registered in an African state, managed by a majority of African citizens or diaspora, and must derive at least two-thirds of their income from membership contributions.

NGOs with observer status undertake to hold regular consultations with the AU and submit a report every three years on their cooperation with the AU. They have access to the open sessions of summit meetings, and may be invited to participate in sessions of closed meetings relevant to their area of interest. So far, 49 African NGOs have been granted observer status with the AU.

NGOs have called for the amendment of these rules, particularly the requirement that organisations seeking observer status must have two-thirds funding from their own members. CIDO has been tasked to review the observer status procedures.

Criteria to obtain observer status with the African Union:
- Registration in an AU Member State.
- In operation for at least three years.
- A democratically adopted constitution.
- Management made up of a majority of African citizens or members of African diaspora.
- Basic resources derived at least two-thirds from membership contributions
- respect and application of non-discrimination principles.

Application procedure:
- Applications must be submitted six months prior to the Executive Council meetings.
- Diaspora organisations require references from two Member States and an NGO recognised by the AU.
- Organisations working on similar issues are encouraged to apply for observer status as a coalition or joint committee.

Criteria for granting African Union Observer Status to Non-Governmental Organisations (NGOs) available at the AU website:
www.africa-union.org/Summit/JULY%202005/

> Accessing information

The major obstacle to engaging with the AU is the lack of publicly available, up-to-date and useful information. Though the AU website has improved, many documents are not posted there until they are already finalised, too late for civil society organisations to comment on them.

Member States receive summit documents through their embassies in Addis Ababa. Foreign Ministry and embassy officials can therefore be a good source of documents that the AU Commission itself has not yet made available.

The websites and mailing lists in Appendix 3 also provide useful sources of information.

Tips on strategy: Understanding a country's interest in the AU and potential points of leverage

- Know your history and politics! Consider the country's strategic political and economic interests in the AU and on a particular issue. What positions has the government taken and which other Member States has the country worked with or opposed in the past? Tailor your advocacy message with this analysis in mind.

- Find out whether the country takes a strong position on an issue of interest – which may mean that its stance is inflexible. If it has not yet formed a position or has a marginal interest in the issue it may be more open to education, advocacy and influence by NGOs.

- Is the country preparing to host any important upcoming AU meetings or seeking to chair the AU? If so, it may be reluctant to antagonise other Member States or take controversial positions. Alternatively, it may be willing to join coalitions that it would not usually have an interest in, which could give a point of entry.

- Are the country's AU dues fully paid up? If not, it has no voting rights.

- Has the country made any contributions to the AU beyond paying its membership dues, such as supplying troops for peace-keeping operations? If so, it is likely to have an important voice in matters to do with that subject area, and more influence generally.

- Find out about internal processes through which the government prepares for summits and ministerial meetings at national level, including which ministries are likely to be involved in decisions on particular policies. Make contact with those ministries and meet with officials to find out what preliminary positions are prepared, whether they are flexible and how you may be able to influence them. If there is conflict between two ministries, find out which one is most likely to support your view, and provide briefing papers or other materials to help them persuade the others.

- Find out about which parliamentary committee is responsible for the AU and meet with its members to get them interested in the issues that are on the AU agenda and put your viewpoint. Identify the five members of parliament chosen as members of the Pan-African Parliament and maintain contacts with them: they can be a bridge between the continental and national levels for your advocacy.

- Find out which national NGOs and journalists regularly follow the AU – or might be interested in the government's position on particular AU decisions – and brief them on the AU agenda and your priorities.

- When a Head of State is chair of the AU, or a national is a high level official, use the opportunity to: call on the State to ratify all AU conventions and protocols and call for the domestication of these treaties and other relevant legal instruments and policy norms; submit reports, through the relevant PRC committee, on the State's progress in implementing AU decisions at the national level; and raise issues that require the AU's attention with the State's representatives at continental and national level.

> Influencing national-level decisions on AU proposals

Not everything happens at summits themselves.
They are not a true reflection of the AU.
— CSO activist

Every decision taken by the AU must be endorsed by a majority of Member States. Lobbying in national capitals is therefore critical to getting a policy adopted at continental level.

The civil law and common law countries have slightly different institutional structures and traditions in relation to handling of international relations, including the African Union. The civil law countries usually have a legal framework setting out the operational responsibilities of the different government departments, whereas these arrangements tend to be more informal in the common law countries. In all cases, however, the Ministry of Foreign Affairs and the Office of the President play the most important roles. Nearly all Ministries of Foreign Affairs have an Africa, AU or multilateral relations unit.

In addition, the individual ministries responsible for the substantive issues under discussion (justice, health, education, trade, energy, etc.) are consulted about any proposals affecting their responsibilities. They will be invited by the AU to send representatives to the ministerial meetings that discuss and endorse policy documents prepared by an expert group.

The sequence of events for all states in preparing for summits at national level is usually as follows:

CIVIL LAW (FRANCOPHONE AND LUSOPHONE) COUNTRIES

1. The Ministry of Foreign Affairs' AU Branch receives the summit agenda from its mission in Addis Ababa and discusses it with the Legal Affairs Branch, the International Organisations Branch and, according to the importance of the summit, the Ministry's General Secretariat and Office of the Minister.
2. A document incorporating the meeting's output and comments

from the Permanent Representative to the AU are presented to the Minister.

3. The ministry dispatches technical documents to the line ministries for each item on the summit agenda and requests comments.

4. The ministry organises consultations in collaboration with the Office of the President and the relevant departments of the Office of the Prime Minister to prepare fact sheets for each item on agenda that is of interest.

5. A file containing the fact sheets and draft position papers is presented to the minister for approval.

6. The papers are then submitted to the President to obtain his political position on each of the proposals.

7. The permanent representative in Addis Ababa continues to update the ministry on agenda changes and comments on the proposed positions.

8. National position papers for the summit are formally approved by the President after Presidential aides have reviewed it in-depth.

COMMON LAW (ANGLOPHONE / COMMONWEALTH) COUNTRIES

1. The Ministry or Department of Foreign Affairs receives the summit agenda with the AU permanent representative's comments on the positions of other Member States.

2. The document is sent to the AU or Africa Affairs desk, which will be responsible for drafting the briefs.

3. Foreign affairs officials decide which departments and ministries will draft the government position on agenda items.

4. AU or Africa Desk officers meet with government agencies (and sometimes civil society) on an ad hoc basis to discuss specific issues on the summit agenda.

5. AU or Africa Desk officers draw up a draft position paper which is presented to foreign affairs officials for discussion at an inter-departmental meeting. The meeting is chaired by the ministry's permanent secretary or deputy or the department's director general or director.

6. The document is approved by the permanent secretary or director general and signed by the Minister of Foreign Affairs.

7. Documents are distributed to the official delegation in advance of the summit.

In most countries, the processes and mechanisms through which state bodies engage with AU organs and issues are not as well established as for relations with UN agencies. Ad hoc procedures can take the place of established mechanisms, and officials other than the formally designated organs can have more influence in shaping the government position.

NGO Action: Civil society engagement with the Kenyan government on the proposal for a Union Government for Africa

In early 2007, Kenyan civil society groups engaged with the Ministry of Foreign Affairs on the upcoming 9th Ordinary Summit of the African Union of June-July 2007 at which there was to be a 'Grand Debate on the Union Government' (see Part 3) and on the African Charter on Democracy, Elections and Governance adopted by the Assembly of Heads of State and Government of the African Union in January 2007.

A civil society delegation successfully requested an audience with the Permanent Secretary of the Ministry of Foreign Affairs (MFA). During this meeting, this delegation put forth a number of 'asks' including: (i) Would Kenya be one of the first countries to ratify the Charter on Democracy; and (ii) Whether it would be possible to develop a working relationship between the MFA and civil society so as to generate public debate and popularise the idea of the Union Government in Kenya as a prelude to the main AU summit discussion. The civil society delegates also presented the recently launched report *Towards a People Driven African Union*, jointly published by AfriMAP, AFRODAD and Oxfam.

Following the meeting, the MFA provided greater access for civil society to the AU Desk Officer and the Director of Political Affairs. Civil society and officials from the MFA jointly organised a full day conference on the proposal for the Union Government, as well as sharing a platform at public debate and in the media.

AU Summits

AU ordinary summits are held twice a year. Each summit consists of three two-day meetings that always take place in the same sequence. Usually there is a one-day break between these meetings. The PRC meets first, followed by the Executive Council and then the Assembly of Heads of State and Government.

With the exception of opening and closing sessions, attendance at these meetings is restricted to national delegations, representatives of AU organs (including ECOSOCC), and AU Commission staff.

As a rule, the January summit takes place at the AU headquarters in Addis Ababa. The June–July summit is held in a different Member State each year (often that of the chair of the AU). The AU can also convene extraordinary summits at the request of the Chairperson or a Member State approved by a two-thirds majority of the Member States.

Both the Executive Council and the Assembly can adopt decisions that are binding on Member States, the AU Commission or any one of the AU organs. Some decisions also request the UN and other international bodies to assist the efforts of the AU or African governments.

The agenda for an ordinary session of the Assembly is in principle drawn up by the Executive Council. In practice, the PRC, led by the 15-member bureau, draws up the agenda for summit meetings.

Other AU organs also hold official side meetings during summits, such as:
> the Peace and Security Council
> the African Peer Review Forum
> the NEPAD Heads of State and Government Implementation Committee

OFFICIAL PRE-SUMMIT MEETINGS FOR CIVIL SOCIETY ORGANISATIONS

Women's Forum: The AU Commission's Women, Gender and Development Directorate organises a pre-summit women's consultation in collaboration with women's organisations, including coalitions such as Solidarity for African Women's Rights (SOAWR) and the Gender Is My Agenda campaign coordinated by Femmes Africa Solidarité. The meeting focuses on mainstreaming gender in AU policies and programmes and the implementation of the Protocol to the African Charter on the Rights of Women in Africa and the Solemn Declaration on Gender Equality in Africa.

CSO Forum: The office of CIDO in the AU Commission organises meetings for selected civil society organisations prior to some summits. The agenda may include a briefing on AU developments and the key issues to be tabled at a summit. The meetings provide an opportunity for a limited number of civil society groups to make recommendations on issues to be discussed at summits.

ACCREDITATION TO SUMMITS

Accreditation to a summit is a separate process from obtaining observer status with the AU. It is not necessary to have observer status to be accredited to a summit.

Accreditation starts three months before a summit. If the summit is taking place elsewhere than Addis Ababa, the host government will usually establish a separate website with protocol information and application forms. This information will also be posted on the AU website.

There are four types of accreditation.

> Delegate – governments of Member States
> Observer – NGOs, non-African governments, UN agencies
> Staff – host government and AU Commission
> Media – national and international press

Civil society organisations wishing to obtain accreditation to a summit should request accreditation from CIDO (cido@africa-union.org) 3 months before the Summit. The request should mention the reasons why the organization wants to participate in the summit. Other AU Directorates and

Departments may also forward the names of selected organisations to be accredited as observers. The Secretary to the Commission draws up the final invitation list. However, even without accreditation, lobbying with delegates may be possible outside the confines of the specific summit venue.

Two types of badges are required at summits. One is a security badge bearing your photograph. The other type indicates the meetings which you can attend. A photo will be taken in the accreditation room then badges are prepared. This will usually take at least one day.

COMMUNICATING WITH DELEGATIONS

You have to do the legwork because no one else will do it for you.
— Civil society activist

Observer status at a summit does not give speaking rights, or even the right to attend more than the opening and closing ceremonies of the Executive Council and Assembly sessions. However, lobbying is often possible in the corridors of the meeting venue. The PRC and Executive Council meetings may be more productive to engage with than the Assembly itself, by which time the major decisions have already been taken or are at Head of State level only.

If the summit is in Addis Ababa, documents and meeting invitations can be distributed to the national embassies of individual countries. At summits taking place in other capitals, there is often a Member State mailbox system, through which invitations to press conferences, book launches and other events can be distributed.

Only the Head of State and three other delegates may attend the Assembly sessions themselves. However, it is common practice for Member States to bring larger delegations of officials from the Ministry of Foreign Affairs and the Office of the President. These delegates can attend other meetings such as the Peace and Security Council or the NEPAD Implementation Committee (or civil society events). Ministers and ministry officials from line ministries relevant to the summit theme or agenda topics are also often part of the delegation. Different delegates may be present during different parts of the summit.

Civil society organisations are not usually included in official delegations, but there are sometimes exceptions: for example, Mali included women's organisations in its delegation at the Maputo summit in 2003, where the

Protocol to the African Charter on the Rights of Women was adopted; also Ghana and Kenya included civil society representatives in their official delegation for the June–July 2007 Accra summit.

MEDIA FACILITIES AT SUMMITS

The AU Commission and the Information Ministry of the host country are responsible for press accreditation. The AU Commission organises a press centre at the summit venue, offering internet facilities, daily press briefings and press kits.

The Pan-African Press Agency produces a daily bulletin during the AU summits. The African Press Agency also reports extensively on proceedings.

> www.panapress.com
> www.apanews.net

NGO Action: The Centre for Citizens' Participation in the African Union

The Centre for Citizens' Participation in the African Union (CCP-AU) was established in 2007 as an independent platform committed to the actualisation of a people-driven African Union. CCP-AU aspires to broaden and strengthen opportunities for substantive AU-CSO engagement.

The CCP-AU was established with the mandate to coordinate and facilitate the existing activities of pan-African civil society organisations, and to encourage other organisations around the continent to engage with the AU and inform the people of Africa about the AU decision-making process.

From 2007 to 2009, the CCP-AU held training workshops for more than 100 representatives of African civil society organisations on the structure of the AU and how to engage it. During the same period, the CCP-AU organised five continental conferences that gathered over 350 CSOs' representatives from all over the continent to engage the AU bi-annual summits. Those continental conferences resulted in concrete recommendations, which were compiled into communiqués distributed to all delegations attending and media covering the summits.

E-mail: aucitizens@yahoo.com
Website: www.ccpau.org

Tips on strategy: Organising for an AU summit

Identify organisations potentially interested in the AU and the decisions to be made at the summit.

- If you wish to hold a side-event in the margins of the summit, liaise early on with CIDO, ECOSOCC, and other organisations already familiar with the relevant processes, as well as with groups that may want to collaborate on a shared event to maximise impact. Freedom to hold side events varies according to the country in which the summit is held.

- Convene open meetings among interested civil society groups at least two months before the summit to generate an exchange of views and perspectives on upcoming decisions.

- Request meetings for a delegation with the Ministry of Foreign Affairs to obtain a briefing on the government's positions and advocate for the concerns of civil society groups.

- Contact Pan-African organisations and offer to work with them.

- Make a media contact list of national, continental and international media likely to attend the summit, and brief journalists on the key issues and the most important civil society representatives for them to talk to.

- Prepare a press briefing note on critical issues and the AU's role in influencing them.

When a state is hosting an AU summit, organise a national civil society committee to request:

- Civil society representation in the inter-ministerial task force that oversees summit arrangements.

- A CSO work centre with Internet and meeting facilities close to where the summit is being held.

- Transparency in the accreditation for observer status and visas for national and visiting CSOs.

- Accommodation for visiting CSOs to include discount rates enjoyed by official delegates.

- Inclusion of CSO meetings in the delegate handbook, the delegate pack and the official website.

NGO Action: Civil society activism at summits for African positions on HIV and AIDS, TB and Malaria

At two extraordinary summits held in Abuja, Nigeria, in 2000 and 2001, African Heads of State agreed to ambitious Declarations and Plans of Action on Malaria and on HIV and AIDS, Tuberculosis and Other Infectious Diseases. They committed to raising health expenditures to 15 per cent of national budgets. Five years later only Botswana and the Gambia had met the target. Fifteen countries, most of them in West and Central Africa, allocated less than 5 per cent of their budgets to health. Only 18 countries allocated more than 10 per cent.

Against this background, the Africa Public Health Rights Alliance launched the 15 per cent Now! Campaign to challenge governments to meet the Abuja target. The Alliance intends to advance Africans' right to health by advocating that governments end Africa's health worker shortage immediately and honour their commitment to the 2001 Abuja Declaration. In January 2007, Nobel Peace laureates Archbishop Desmond Tutu and Prof Wangari Maathai added their voices to this appeal to Heads of State attending the African Union summit to meet their pledge to allocate 15 per cent of national budgets to health care.

African Public Health Rights Alliance: http://www.worldaidscampaign.org/en/In-country-campaigns/Sub-Saharan-Africa/A-Background-15-Now!-Campaign

The African Civil Society Coalition on HIV and AIDS was formed to mobilise an effective advocacy response to key global meetings around AIDS that took place during 2006, including the UN General Assembly Special Session (UNGASS) on HIV and AIDS held in June of that year. The coalition formed a Pan-African steering committee and a month later negotiated with the AU Commission's Directorate of Social Affairs for invitations to a series of health-related meetings. In addition to mobilising the participation of a large number of African NGOs to participate in the UNGASS, the Coalition played a significant role in positively influencing the outcomes of the Special Summit of the African Union on AIDS, TB and Malaria that was held in Abuja, Nigeria 2–4 May 2006. The Coalition's participation and lobbying resulted in the commitments on regional targets, strong roles for civil society and parliamentarians, and comprehensive language contained in the African Common Position and the Abuja Call for Accelerated Action, two of the outcome documents from the summit.

UNAIDS Director Dr Peter Piot later praised the coalition for raising the international visibility of African CSOs. The coalition provided an example to be emulated in other regions of the world, he said.

African CSO Coalition on HIV and AIDS:
http://www.worldaidscampaign.org/en/In-country-campaigns/Sub-Saharan-Africa

Part Three

The Union Government Debate

Since the OAU was founded there has been debate among Member States over the framework for continental institutions and the balance between political and economic integration and national sovereignty. The early drive for a 'Union Government' for Africa led by President Kwame Nkrumah of Ghana was defeated at the 1965 Accra summit of the OAU, and a quarter-century later the 1991 Abuja Treaty establishing the AEC endorsed a 'gradualist' approach, creating a distant time-table for the achievement of full integration. However, some Member States – and some African citizens – continued to lobby for integration to progress more rapidly. These debates contributed to the establishment of the African Union to replace the OAU – and have if anything become more noisy since the AU Constitutive Act was adopted.

Pressure for a more integrationist legal framework for the AU led to the appointment of a committee of seven Heads of State, who presented a report to the July 2006 Banjul summit. The AU Commission was then mandated to produce a more detailed report on the issues, and produced a 'Study on Union Government: Towards a United States of Africa', presented to the January 2007 Addis Ababa summit. The Assembly then decided that there would be one central theme and agenda item at the Accra summit in July 2007, a 'Grand Debate on the Union Government'.

Ahead of the Accra summit, members of the PRC and Executive Council met in May for a retreat, culminating in an extraordinary session of Ministers of Foreign Affairs, in Durban, South Africa, where the Union Government proposals were discussed. The delegations did not reach consensus.

The Assembly discussed the Union Government at the Accra summit on 1–3 July 2007. The 'Accra Declaration' noted the need for common responses to the challenges of globalisation, for a consensus on shared values, and for the involvement of Africa's people and the African diaspora in the debate. In a compromise between those states that wanted to move quickly to the creation of a 'United States of Africa' and those that were more cautious, the Assembly agreed to accelerate the economic and political integration of the African continent, and accelerate the rationalisation of the RECs, and also to conduct an audit of the institutions and organs of the AU to review the challenges they already faced and make proposals on how best to move forward. A ministerial committee was appointed to work on these issues.

A panel of eminent persons was set up to conduct the 'Audit Review' and presented a long and detailed report to the January 2008 summit on the functioning of the existing AU organs. Among the many recommendations made were that:

> The **Assembly** should return to one annual meeting of Heads of State and the term of the Chairperson should be two years.
> The **Executive Council** should be renamed the Council of Ministers and be composed sectorally, with different ministers attending according to what is on the agenda.
> The **Commission** should be reorganised to strengthen the authority of the chairperson. The chair and deputy chair should be elected six months ahead of the rest of the commissioners, and the chair should assign portfolios to the individual commissioners.
> **Implementation of AU decisions** should be improved by ensuring that the first item on the agenda of each Assembly session is a review of previous decisions, by the establishment of National Commissions on AU Affairs and by the imposition of sanctions for noncompliance.

At the January and July 2008 summits, the Assembly decided to postpone decisions once again. In January 2008, the election of a new Chairperson and Commissioners of the AU Commission went ahead according to the previous system, and the Assembly appointed a Committee of Twelve Heads of State and Government (Botswana, Cameroon, Egypt, Ethiopia, Gabon, Ghana, Libya, Nigeria, Senegal, South Africa, Tanzania and Uganda) to review the proposals made by the audit review. At the July 2008 summit, the Assembly requested the AU Commission to present a report on the modalities for implementing the recommendations of the Committee of Twelve to the February 2009 Assembly, 'with a view to bringing the debate to a final conclusion' at that meeting.

At a special session of the Assembly held on 1 February 2009, however, the Assembly decided only to transform the AU Commission into an AU Authority, with strengthened resources and powers, and to refer further decisions (such as a proposed reorganisation of departments) once again to the next summit after further study of the necessary amendments to the Constitutive Act by an Extraordinary Session of the Executive Council. The Executive Council met in Libya during April 2009, to consider the functions of the new AU Authority, the size of the Authority, the functions of the secretaries who would head the new departments, and the financial implications of establishing the Authority.

The Conclusions of the Executive Council Extraordinary Session were modest. Ministers endorsed an expansion of the areas of competence of the AU Authority, which will replace the AU Commission, but left the structure of the Authority mostly unchanged from that of the Commission and did not follow the recommendations of the AU Audit Review to strengthen the powers of the chairperson. The Extraordinary Session also emphasised that the AU is 'a Union of independent and sovereign States; as such, it is an inter-governmental organisation and all its organs are of an inter-governmental nature. In all cases, the Assembly shall retain its right to delegate any function and/or power to any organ of the Union including the Authority'. The Authority has, however, been given the role of coordinating the AU position on key issues. These conclusions were endorsed by the Assembly during the June–July 2009 summit, also held in Libya.

The long delays in finalising the proposals for the restructuring of the AU reflect not only technical differences about the best way of configuring the secretariat for the African Union and the powers that should be given to its different organs, but also philosophical differences among African leaders about the future direction for the continent, including concerns about the role for state sovereignty in a more integrated Africa. The drive for greater African integration is welcomed by almost all Africans, but some also fear that the creation of new institutions without broad consultation among Africa's peoples could result in less rather than more space for democratic participation in the work of the premier continental body.

African civil society organisations and parliaments need to engage in this debate. Fundamental questions remain unresolved about the structure and reach of Africa's continental institutions and the degree of protection for national sovereignty. The revisions of the Constitutive Act that are underway provide opportunities for advocacy on issues such as when and how the AU structures may intervene in a Member State; on the priorities among the various challenges the continental structures should address; on the relationships among the AU executive organs and between these organs and the Pan-African Parliament; on the participation of civil society in the activities of the executive organs, including especially the PRC; on the legislative authority of the Pan-African Parliament, the system by which its members are chosen, and the participation of civil society in its work; and on the structure of ECOSOCC and its relations both with the AU executive organs and with other civil society organisations. These issues are too important to be left to technocrats and governments.

NGO Action: Lobbying on the Union Government

Civil society access to the debate about the Union Government has been limited, though organisations have mobilised to discuss the proposals at meetings in the margins of the AU summits held in Accra in 2007 and since that date.

Speaking at a GCAP forum on trade and continental integration in Accra during the summit, GCAP Africa Coordinator Christophe Zoungrana commented:

> Like most African civil society organisations, we support the acceleration of the political and economic integration of Africa as a genuine way to development, and therefore we welcome the opportunity of a Union Government for raising the bar for human rights, good governance, and the movement of people and goods across the continent.
>
> However, we should be extremely cautious in promoting deeper and faster political and economic integration of the continent when African citizens are not informed and most existing African Union policies and Regional Economic Communities are not properly implemented. The road to an African Union Government should be democratic and participatory and run alongside the strengthening of past agreements and regional institutions.

AfriMAP made a submission to the 'Audit Review' of the AU institutions, based on the report *Towards a People-Driven African Union: Current Obstacles and New Opportunities* (January 2007, updated November 2007) prepared in collaboration with Oxfam and AFRODAD, as did several other groups. AfriMAP's submission argued that:

> The critical finding from our work with a broad range of civil society organisations interested in engaging with the AU is the need for the AU institutions to be far more open to organisations and individuals who are not government officials, members of the AU Commission, or the small group of insider-outsiders who have privileged access because of their efforts to build up personal contacts in order to gain an understanding of AU processes. Looking forward, the loudly expressed view is that any new institutions and structures established at continental level should enhance the democratic accountability of the AU and empower Africa's citizens and communities, and not just its governments. This will require not only the vision of greater political and economic integration among Africa's states, but steps to increase participation in AU decision-making, as well as a clear focus on creating effective institutions that can implement and enforce the decisions that they take.

GCAP: www.whiteband.org
AfriMAP: www.afrimap.org/researchDetail.php?id=33

Appendices

Appendix 1: AU Regions

The Member States of the five regions of the AU are as follows:

EAST
Comoros, Djibouti, Ethiopia, Eritrea, Kenya, Madagascar, Mauritius, Rwanda, Somalia, Seychelles, Sudan, Tanzania, Uganda.

CENTRAL
Burundi, Cameroon, Central African Republic, Chad, Democratic Republic of Congo, Republic of Congo, Equatorial Guinea, Gabon, São Tomé and Príncipe.

NORTH
Algeria, Egypt, Libya, Mauritania, Sahrawi Arab Democratic Republic, Tunisia.

SOUTH
Angola, Botswana, Lesotho, Malawi, Mozambique, Namibia, South Africa, Swaziland, Zambia, Zimbabwe.

WEST
Benin, Burkina Faso, Cabo Verde, Côte d'Ivoire, Gambia, Ghana, Guinea-Bissau, Guinea, Liberia, Mali, Nigeria, Niger, Senegal, Sierra Leone, Togo.

Appendix 2: Regional Economic Communities recognised by the African Union

REC	Member States	Objectives	Activities/Programmes
Arab Maghreb Union (UMA) www.maghrebarabe.org	Algeria, Libya, Mauritania, Morocco,* Tunisia	• Promote trade and economic cooperation	Infrastructure, Security, food safety
Common Market for Eastern and Southern Africa (COMESA) www.comesa.int	Burundi, Comoros, Democratic Republic of the Congo, Djibouti, Egypt, Eritrea, Ethiopia, Kenya, Libya, Madagascar, Malawi, Mauritius, Rwanda, Seychelles, Sudan, Swaziland, Uganda, Zambia, Zimbabwe	• Attain trade and economic cooperation • Promote peace and security in the region	Trade and investment, trade liberalisation and facilitation, Agriculture and food, Private Sector Support, infrastructure, Women In business, Peace and security, multilateral negotiations, Monetary Harmonisation
Community of Sahel-Saharan States (CEN-SAD) www.cen-sad.org	Benin, Burkina Faso, Central African Republic, Chad, Cote d'Ivoire, Djibouti, Egypt, Eritrea, Gambia, Ghana, Guinea Bissau, Kenya, Liberia, Libya, Mali, Morocco, Niger, Nigeria, Senegal, Sierra Leone, Somalia, Sudan, Togo, Tunisia	• Strengthen peace, security and stability • Achieve global economic and social development	Agriculture, industry, energy, trade liberalisation, transport and communication, education, security
East African Community (EAC) www.eac.int	Burundi, Kenya, Rwanda, Tanzania, Uganda	• Attain socio-economic cooperation, development and integration • Maintain peace and security • Attain political federation	Trade liberalisation, natural resources management, peace and security, energy, infrastructure, environmental management, science and technology
Economic Community of Central African States (ECCAS) www.ceeac-eccas.org	Angola, Burundi, Cameroon, Chad, Central African Republic, Democratic Republic of Congo, Equatorial Guinea, Gabon, Republic of Congo, Rwanda, São Tomé and Príncipe	• Achieve collective autonomy and maintain economic stability • Develop capacities to maintain peace and security • Attain economic and monetary integration	Peace and security, Agriculture, energy cooperation, natural resources cooperation, tourism, trade liberalisation, industrial development, transport and communications, science and technology

REC	Member States	Objectives	Activities/Programmes
Economic Community of West African States (ECOWAS) www.ecowas.int	Benin, Burkina Faso, Cape Verde, Cote d'Ivoire, Gambia, Ghana, Guinea, Guinea Bissau, Liberia, Mali, Niger, Nigeria, Senegal, Sierra Leone, Togo	• Achieve social political interactions, economic cooperation, integration and shared development	Agriculture, Economic and Monetary Affairs, Education and Training, Health and Social affairs, Energy, Environment, Trade, food Security, Defence and Security, humanitarian interventions, ICT, Infrastructure, Rural Development, Telecommunications, Trade, Transport and water
Intergovernmental Authority on Development (IGAD) www.igad.org	Djibouti, Eritrea, Ethiopia, Kenya, Somalia, Sudan, Uganda	• Attain regional economic cooperation and integration • Promote regional security and political dialogue • Promote trade and social economic development and cooperation	Conflict Prevention, Management and Resolution and Humanitarian Affairs; Infrastructure development (Transport and Communications); Food Security and Environment Protection
Southern African Development Community (SADC) www.sadc.int	Angola, Botswana, DRC, Lesotho, Madagascar, Malawi, Mauritius, Mozambique, Namibia, Seychelles, South Africa, Swaziland, Tanzania, Zambia, Zimbabwe	• Cooperation and integration in the socio economic arena, as well as political development	Food, Agriculture and Natural Resources, Trade, Industry, Finance and Investment, Infrastructure and Services, Social and Human Development

Source: AU Audit Review

* Morocco withdrew from the OAU in 1984 when the Sahrawi Arab Democratic Republic was admitted as a member.

Appendix 3: Useful websites and contacts

OFFICIAL WEBSITES:

> **African Union**
> www.africa-union.org
> **Pan-African Parliament**
> www.pan-african-parliament.org
> **NEPAD**
> www.nepad.org
> **APRM**
> www.aprm-international.org

OTHER SOURCES OF INFORMATION ON THE AU:

> **Institute for Security Studies**: www.issafrica.org
> Follow links to African Organisations from the home page for a
> comprehensive database of documents issued by the AU and by
> the regional economic communities.
> **AU Monitor**: www.pambazuka.org/aumonitor/
> News stories and commentary on developments relating to the
> AU and Africa's relations with the rest of the world, with option
> to subscribe to bilingual weekly compilation by email.
> **AfriMAP**: www.afrimap.org
> News stories focusing on the APRM, African integration and
> governance in Africa, as well as a collection of African norms and
> standards in both English and French.
> **Centre for Citizens Participation in the AU**: www.ccpau.org
> Information for civil society interested in the AU, with option to
> subscribe to AU citizens mailing list.